Stolen Love

Poetry For Cheaters

D. Reid Wallace

WISE PRESS ◉ NEW YORK

Copyright © 1998 by M. Cecile Forté

All rights reserved including the right of
reproduction in whole or in part in any form.

Wise Press
Port Jefferson Station, New York

Manufactured in the United States of America

Wallace, D. Reid
Stolen Love: Poetry For Cheaters/D. Reid Wallace.

ISBN: 0-9652823-1-7

All photographs used by permission:
Comstock Photo Archives, New York

Book Design: Fleury Design

Table of Contents

Foreword

Introduction

Stolen Love
- 3 -

In the beginning...

Brand New
- 7 -

Thrilling
- 9 -

Know That I'm Out Here For A Good Time
- 13 -

Peanut Butter Chocolate
- 17 -

Share-A-Man Plan
- 19 -

The He In Me
- 23 -

Hello, Again
- 27 -

In the middle...

Manspeak
- 31 -

My Psychic Says
- 33 -

Understand
- 35 -

Don't Start!
- 41 -

Still...
- 43 -

Bad Boy and Good Man
- 47 -

A Woman Like You
- 49 -

The Difference
- 51 -

Does he notice...?
- 53 -

Holidays and Weekends
- 57 -

20 lbs.
- 59 -

Younger Woman/Younger Man
- 63 -

Not Guilty Enough
- 65 -

It's
- 67 -

A Year From Now
- 71 -

In the end...

With You In The Room It's Even More Empty
- 75 -

Can't Cheat A Cheater
- 79 -

Heartburn
- 83 -

Next Lifetime
- 87 -

Disconnected
- 89 -

"...but you're my best friend!"
- 93 -

Last Best Day
- 95 -

Promised Land
- 99 -

Foreword

If prostitution is the oldest profession, then cheating must be the oldest sport. From William Shakespeare to Nathaniel Hawthorne to Tennessee Williams to Robert Waller, it is the delicious taboo that sets the page on fire and sizzles on screen. At a time when the dalliances of celebrities, politicians and the neighbor next door are the subject of everyday conversation, it seems reasonable to believe that there might be a need for an uncommon perspective.

This collection of more than two dozen poems makes no judgments, points no fingers, offers no easy way to come to grips with betrayal. What it does offer is creative expression and entertainment for those who experience these relationships as well as those who do not.

It is not literary, just ideas strung together in plain, rhythmic words I hope the reader will find pleasing. It is the work of a student of popular culture designed to fill an unmet need:

    Clandestine lovers need poetry, too!

Introduction

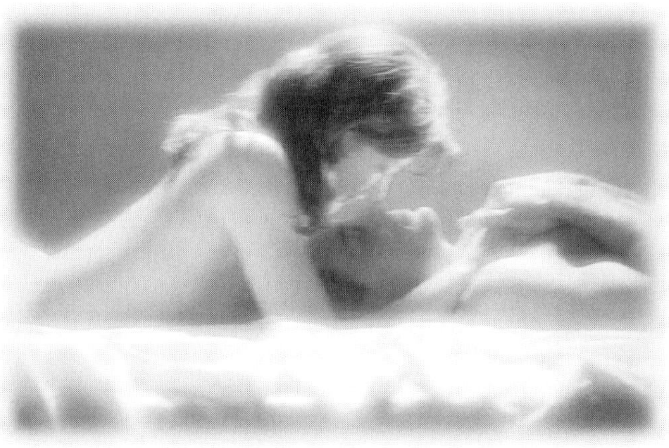

Stolen Love

What can be said about it,
What answers can we presume?
One thing's for certain:
It's what you're not getting at home.
Arousal? Impossible after awhile
But, in a strange bed
There's pleasure ahead
The stream of life easily flows through.
How can you put that intensity up against
What's all too familiar to you?

Perhaps marriage isn't meant to be a fairy tale
Likely doomed, it appears, to grow old and stale
The foreign born may have it right in arranging matrimonial ties,
Marriage has a hard time holding passion's heat
Cools off eventually, leaving room for lies and deceit.

Maybe we expect too much, but whatever the cause may be
Mystery of mysteries
It goes back to when time began,
An eternal secret adventure for both
Woman and man.

The deeper issues of love it seems we understand
To care for, protect, support and
Be there day to day
Raising families, being part of communities
Are what we value, or so we say.
But somehow intense heat and sweet passion
Encountered between strange sheets
Wear away at our sincerest efforts not to become hypocrites.

An answer? Don't think there's one I or anyone can claim
Stolen love's a human hobby seemingly impossible to tame.

Western wind, when wilt thou blow,
The small rain down can rain?
Christ, if my love were in my arms
And I in my bed again!

— *Oxford Book of 16th Century Verse*

Sigh no more, ladies, sigh no more,
Men were deceivers ever;
One foot in sea, and one on shore;
To one thing constant never;
Then sigh not so,
But let them go,
And be you blithe and bonny;
Converting all your sounds of woe
Into Hey nonny, nonny.

— William Shakespeare,
Much Ado About Nothing, Act II, Scene III

We are the music-makers,
And we are the dreamers of dreams,
Wandering by lone sea breakers,
And sitting by desolate streams;
World-losers and world-forsakers,
On whom the pale moon gleams:
Yet we are the movers and shakers
Of the world forever, it seems.

— Arthur O'Shaughnessy

In the beginning...

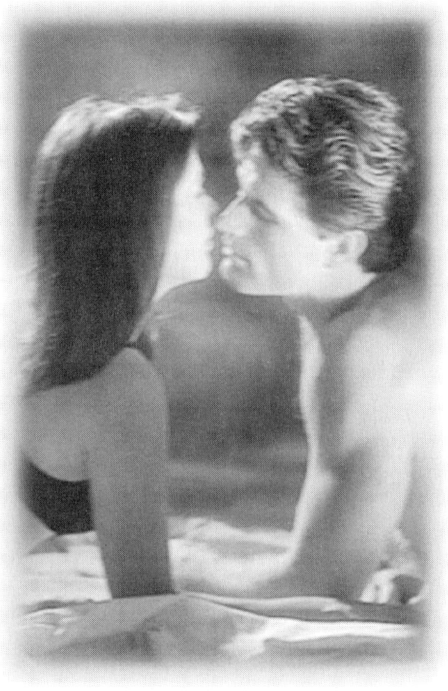

Brand New

It's only been a little while and already I can say
Whether you're right here at my side, or away doing what you do
Everything looks brighter, I feel more alive, as if I'm
Brand new.
Thank you.

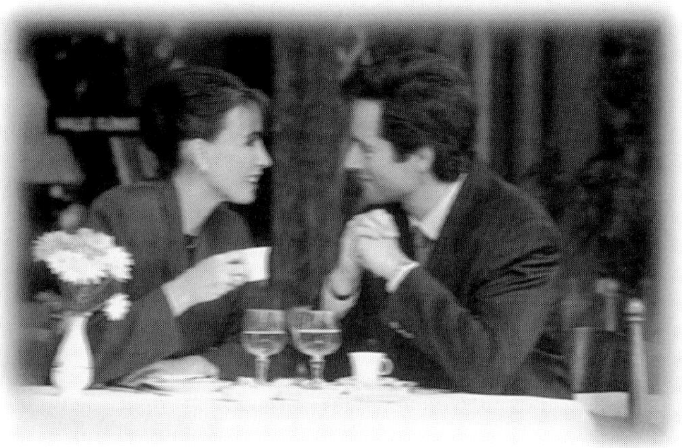

Thrilling

Breathless phrases squeezed from throats dry with excitement
Hearts pounding a higher volume than words
Full sentences requiring concentration
But falling victim to silent understanding.

Not looking – just going about the day's business
Our eyes said. Couldn't have known
Such a feeling would overtake us
Make us notice someone new
That ordinary day.

Was it sincere compliment
Or some less than clever pick-up line?
No matter, I smiled
Passed by
Embarrassed, silenced by the unexpected attention
That ordinary day.

What was it about me that pushed his thoughts into words?
No matter, he'd take the time to learn
Everything I had to teach
His goal within reach
That ordinary day.

Deliberate moves long denied allowed us a second look
Into chocolate eyes, at shy smiles
Lingering a moment longer
A sameness of desire showing shameless
In our gaze
Turning
Ordinary to extraordinary.

If there's crime in this, it's that delicious, instant desire
To do wrong that sometimes comes
On ordinary days.

I have loved many, the more and the few
I have loved many that I might love you.

— Grace Fallow Norton
Song of the Sum of All

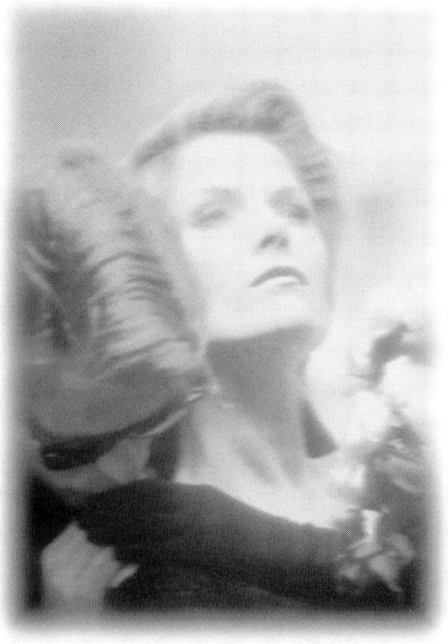

Know That I'm Out Here For A Good Time

I'm selfish enough to pursue
What it'll take to date you
I know you're a married woman, you know I'm a married man
Can you accept the fact that
I'm out here for a good time?

Yes, my wife does understand me and no, what we have hasn't
Lost its spark
I just can't help myself, you're too beautiful
But you can never have my heart
I'm being as up front as I can
I'm a married man
Out for a good time.

Don't think that I'm some challenge – a man
You seek to change
Don't take the pretty words I say, analyze and rearrange
Them to mean more than they do
Think of it as fantasy, sexual excitement for two
I've been here before
And I want nothing more than
A good time.

You may think I'm too blunt and blame me
I'm just speaking what's all true
Believe me, it's really the best thing that I could do for you
I never want you to say you didn't
Know that I was out for a good time.

Take courage, my beloved daughter;
take courage.
Have a just confidence in yourself
and in your husband.
For a moment he may be fascinated
by the arts of an unprincipled woman;
for a moment she may triumph
over his senses and his imagination;
but of his esteem, his affection, his heart,
she cannot rob you.

— Maria Edgeworth
Leonora, Letter XXVII

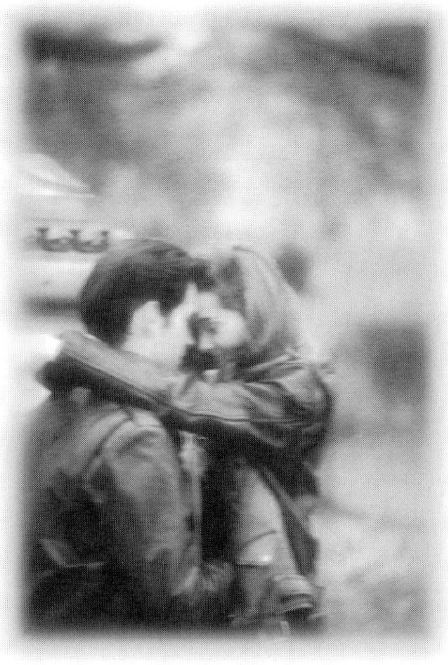

Peanut Butter Chocolate

Peanut butter chocolate
Adores it, I heard him say
Found a little store
That makes it homemade
The other day.

When I handed it to him
He was so surprised,
You should have seen
The look of happiness
In his eyes
At the sight of
Peanut butter chocolate.

A simple thing like that
Makes my special
Someone smile
Pleases me to please him
With surprises
Once in a while.
So I've decided to start
A "Keeping Sweetheart Happy" file:

Peanut butter chocolate for him
His good loving for me
Mix well and serve
One perfect
Clandestine lover's recipe.

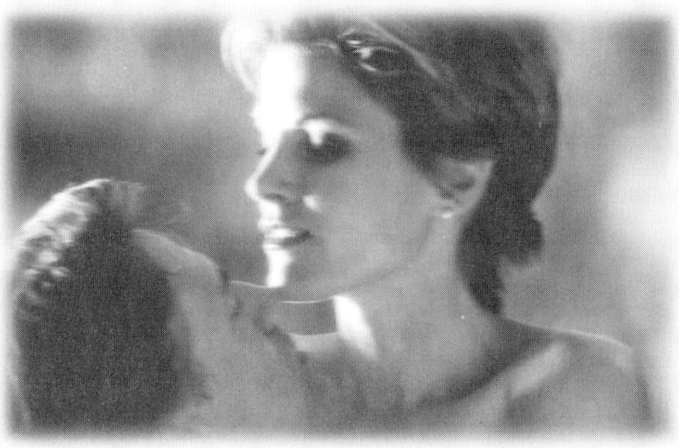

Share-A-Man Plan
(for Dahlia)

An old woman told me about the plan
She was wise enough never to keep a man
In her house or in her heart,
Never to start growing weary of his touch
Or thinking too much about where he's been
Or where he's going when he's alone, on his own.

She clamped her long stiff fingers on my shoulder, cocked her head and said,
"She owns him, and you get to rent him
Every once in a while," then she smiled.
"But I want a man of my own!" I intoned. With sarcasm she replied,
"Excuse me, Miss True Blue, then it wouldn't do for you
To engage in the share-a-man plan."

"That plan's an excuse for abuse against another
Sisterwoman, how can you offer such advice?
It's just not nice. And from a lady your age!"
She giggled with glee, then turning on me she said,
"Look here girly girl, life's gonna curl those toes of
Yours one day. And if he's not free, you'll begin to
Think like me, as you tire of a frog that's no prince.
Time and longing will convince
You to start working the share-a-man plan."
"It's to be despised, it's just not civilized!
Never," I swore, believing more in justice than some
Ol' woman's advice. I was above love's thievery.

But one day I stole away to paradise with someone very nice;
Married with kids, sex on the skids
Lots of comfort at home but no heat.
Happily stealing love, our passion soaring above the hours of late afternoon.
Soon I forgot all about justice, just us.

Nonetheless we're not free, and it still bothers me
That I'm sharing someone else's man.
Maybe some day I'll put away this lousy plan:
When they can clone the one that she owns
And I have one of him all to myself,
I'll keep my vow and allow her husband to go on home!

...in modern usage, a cuckhold
is the husband of an unfaithful wife —
a far nastier and more humiliating state,
apparently, than being the wife of a philanderer,
for which in fact no word exists.

— Anne Fausto-Sterling
Myths of Gender

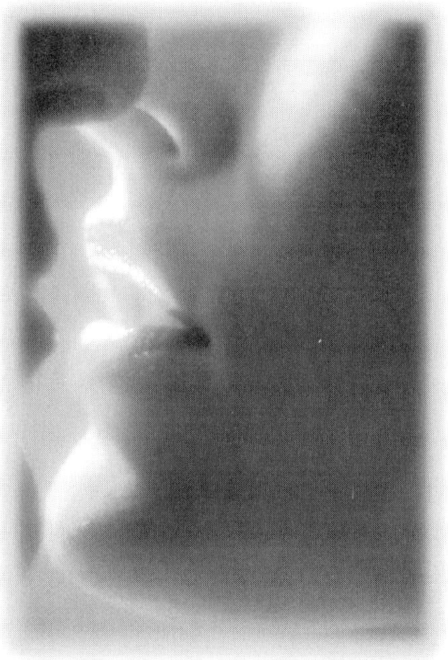

The He In Me

The he in me wants to recapture spring
The he in me wants a good looking, sexy young thing
Time passes, makes us older
Desires bolder
Before age
Cuts short the pages
Of my life
The he in me will have his way.

The he in me wants a "no strings" roll in the hay
The he in me wants it now, today
The he in me wants to rock and roll
The he in me has no need to stroll down
Lover's lane
No time for love or pain
Has the he in me.

The he in me needs relaxation away from office demands
The he in me has little time unplanned
The he in me wants sex that's hot and sweet
The he in me knows how to be discreet
The he in me senses hubby's imagining the worst
But he won't dare complain
Since he was the first
To stray
I'm about to make him pay for
The he in him!

Under the November tree
Shelterless and dim.
He did not think me strange or older.
Nor I, him.

— Frances Cornford
All Souls' Night

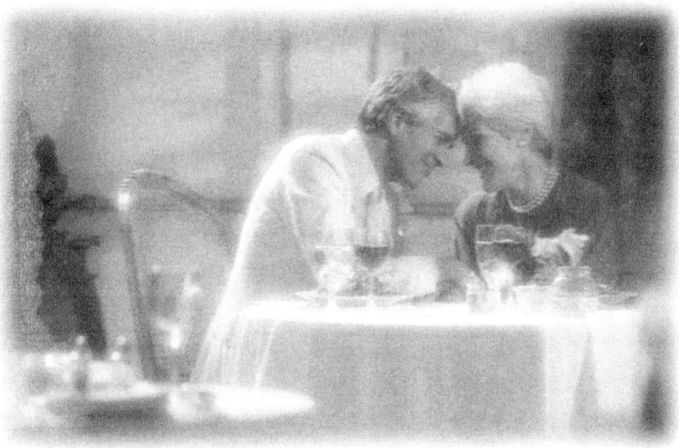

Hello, Again

Your hair has grayed, but your face has kept its youth.
Your gaze makes me know that what I have become still pleases you.
We sip champagne like we once did a lifetime ago in another city,
And you tell me how much you've thought of me, remembering things I'd forgot.
You take it to mean more than it should because I've held on to less;
It's just that I had to erase those memories to go back to living a lie.

This time, teach me to weave this splendor into
The fabric of my life. Teach me to make my time with you beauty, my guilt reason
To be tolerant and kind to the one I once loved more than I will ever love you.
The idea of us is the power that holds me here all over again,
I want, need, and have missed the idea of our secret coupling arousing
All the passion missing in our respective bedrooms.
Was it ever meant to flourish in the orderliness of married life,
Or is its heat sustained instead in chance meetings and wild imaginings
Made so much better in the mind than what is real, what is at hand?

In this way we are one
Woman and man lusting after the same loss.
We are a gift, one to the other. We give the act of life meaning again,
As one, again.

Who needs to remember why we said goodbye so long ago?
Let's just say hello, again.

Had I the heavens' embroidered cloths,
Enwrought with golden and silver light,
The blue and the dim and the dark cloths
Of night and light and the half-light,
I would spread the cloths under your feet:
But I, being poor, have only my dreams;
I have spread my dreams under your feet;
Tread softly because you tread on my dreams.

— William Butler Yeats

Pains of love be sweeter far
Than all other pleasures are.

— John Dryden
Tyrannic Love (1669), act IV, sc. I

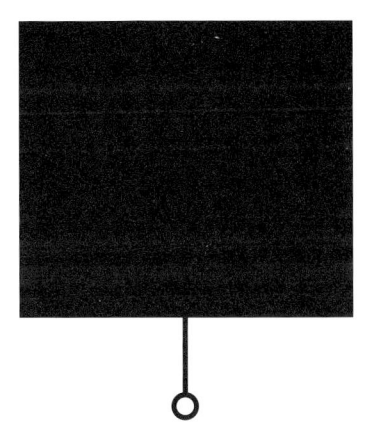

In the middle...

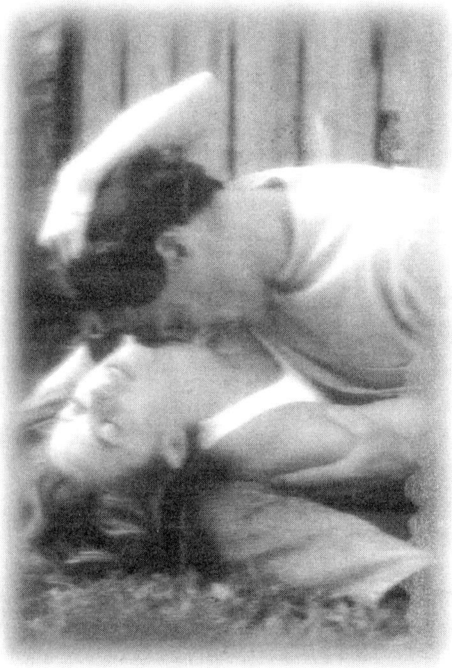

Manspeak

"Deliver me from needy women!" I cried
"They're never freaking satisfied."
They need, they want, they complain all day,
By evening I need to get away
From needy women.

Found this woman whose pleasures are many,
At first, faults she didn't have any.
But now she cares more than she should,
She'd love to hear sweet words from me if she could.

When I call, we talk, her words scratch and sting,
Now you know I don't need this kind of thing!
"A 'love' affair? What's that?
Let's be realistic.
We're consenting adults turning a trick
That's our commitment," is what I said.

But this needy woman cut me some slack,
Sent me a card
Welcomed me back
To her secret garden
Where she shares herself with me in the soft, lusty darkness.
But before long, I'll be gone, having moved on
From this needy woman.

Then it occurred to me in my head
As I lay alone in that hospital bed:
A few sweet words are all I need say
And the needy woman in her will go away.

So I say them when I can remember,
And she blossoms in her secret garden growing ever more tender,
Making it easy to surrender my needs
To a no longer needy woman.

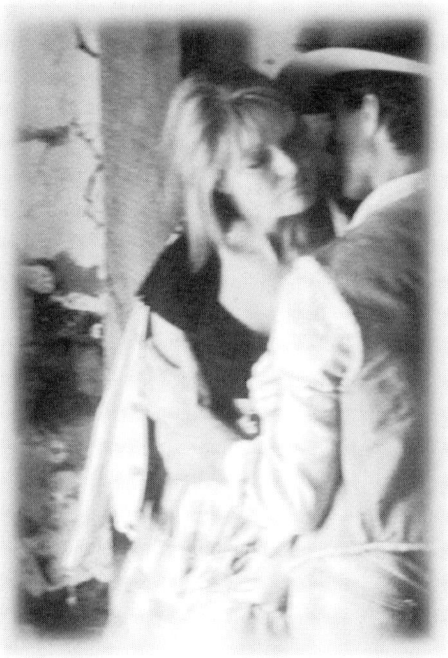

My Psychic Says

My psychic says you're up to no good
Says you've bedded more women than any normal man could
My psychic says you'll hurt me one day and I should stay away
From the likes of you.

My psychic says you're just foolin'
Around with my heart
That I should get smart
About getting in too deep
Stop losing sleep
Over the likes of you.

My psychic says your wife's just fine
In other circumstances she'd be a friend of mine
My psychic says she, too, is often blue
Putting up with the likes of you.

But my psychic doesn't know everything
She doesn't know the thrill
Having you brings
Doesn't know how risking discovery
Makes stealing love with you
Pure reverie.

She can't know because she can't see
How to make her own life better
Never mind me!

So I think I'll ignore her warning and meet you tomorrow morning
Because I couldn't care less about what my psychic says.

By the time you swear you're his,
Shivering and sighing,
And he vows his passion is
Infinite, undying –
Lady make note of this:
One of you is lying.

— Dorothy Parker
Unfortunate Coincidence

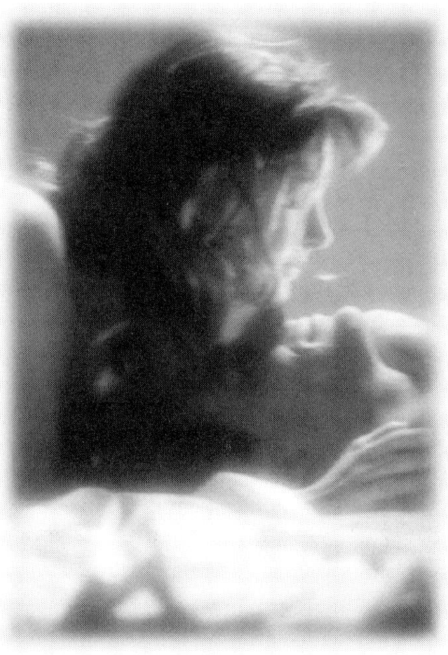

Understand

Now that I've had the chance
To analyze this question of romance,
I understand
What it's going to take and
All that's at stake – in your life, at least.

Along with that, I see
Why you caution against too much
Intimacy: you fear it could ruin your efforts to remain free.
Why not put your trust in me to see how to remedy your fear?
Believe me, I understand.

You openly express
With honesty and power
That you can't shower me with gifts and such;
But I'm in this for so much more:
Affection, attention, the excitement of your touch.
Can't promise I won't take as much as you've got to give!
Surely, you understand.

We've made a pact to keep things sweet,
You can rely on me to be discreet.
Just keep me in your arms and on your mind – a priority
In circumstances of any kind.

Ecstasy awaits,
If you understand.

Everyone knows that...a woman ought not to let it appear that she understands, still less that she believes, the declaration made to her by a lover....

— Margaret of Navarre

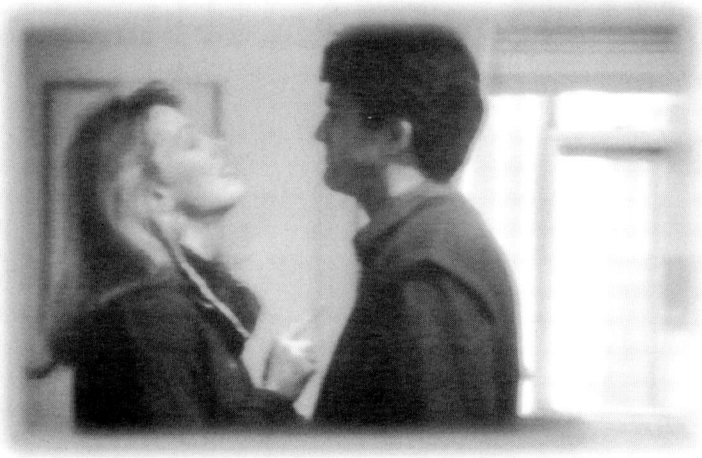

Don't Start!

It's not that I want to upset you but
I can't just let yours the only desires be.
Then what would become of me, Sweetie?
Maybe it's not plain but I hope to gain a measure of
Pleasure from the risk I, too, am taking.
I'm not your wife, with you for life, and
Expected to put up with the hurts and insensitivities
Men like you are prone to.
So please, don't start!

You see, I'm not interested in hearing about her.
Guilt-free cheating won't occur,
Because you keep mentioning her name;
Talking "she" and "we" to me can't free you from blame.
You need to realize – it should come as no surprise
That it makes me ache and causes me to
Aggrevate you with the details of my pain.
There's little to be gained so
Honey, please don't start!

"Why is it when I disagree with you..."
I said, as the phone went dead.
I knew that in your head there was awful me
Giving wonderful you a hard time.
Now you won't take my calls and you refuse my page
Your outrage punishment for my sins.

Yet we both know you'll eventually give in,
And make me smile again
When finally you call and say,
"Now, Sweetheart, don't start!"

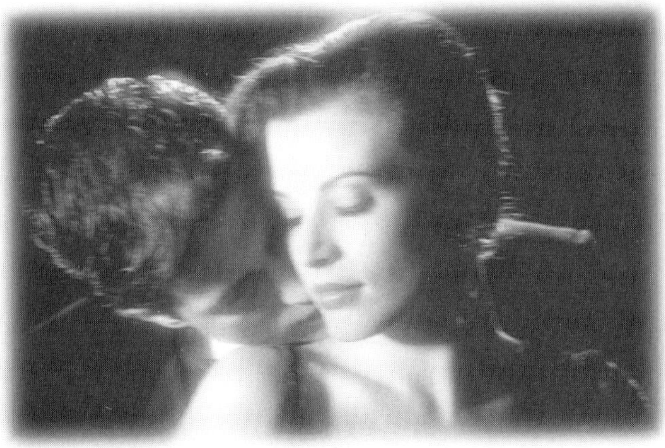

Still...

She cried and I lied as I promised to let you go.
I've hurt her again, seems there's no end to the pain I've caused.
I feel bad, but still...

I can't stay away from you
I'm crazy for your touch, need you so much
You've taken hold of my heart, and still...

She cares for me, in her our children see the ideal mother, and so do I.
I can never deny what she brings to our lives,
She's like all good wives, I'm damn lucky, but still...

I want what's not mine; whenever there's time, I knowingly betray her trust.
I must have you in my life even though
So much of who I am is bound up in
This marriage I once believed was all I needed.

But now the feeling's no longer there, and I don't want to share a life of duty instead.
So I'm selfish enough

To risk it all whenever you call and say you'll see me
Still.

Marriage: a souvenir of love...
One man's folly is another man's wife.

— Helen Rowland
Reflections of a Bachelor Girl 1903

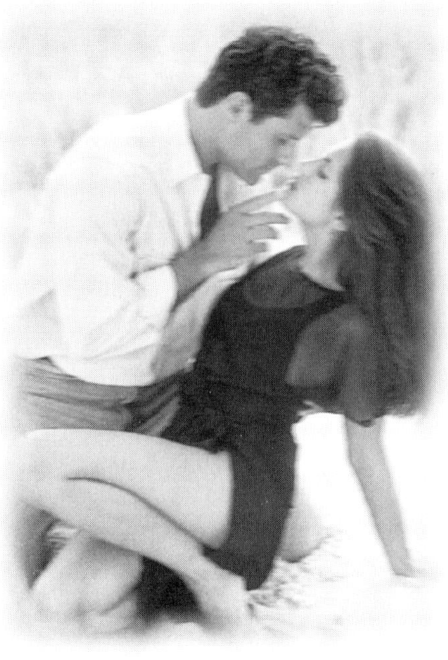

Bad Boy and Good Man

Bad boys don't grow up they grow old
Break your heart and leave you standing in the cold, they say.
Hadn't happened to me that way because
Mine is a good man.

But stories of bold, restless lovers spilled by friends;
Love affairs gone bad, leaving tears, loose ends
Are awfully sad
But oh, what a good time they had
With those very bad boys.

Feeling lucky that I'd avoided such peril
I had no stories of my own to tell;
Just as well
Why borrow trouble?

Of course it didn't stay that way.
A long time married, never strayed
I had no idea that I would meet the one
Who'd put an end to the status quo.

A sleek jungle cat
Dangerous, beautiful and untamed
The murmur of his voice when he calls out my name
As we connect, rise and fall
Over and over again,
Can hardly be described.
Barely able to contend with the web I'm in
Never thought the fire in my soul
Would burn so hot for someone who's
Not the good man I married.

Surely this romance
Will one day come to an end
But until then
There's nothing like loving both bad boy and good man.

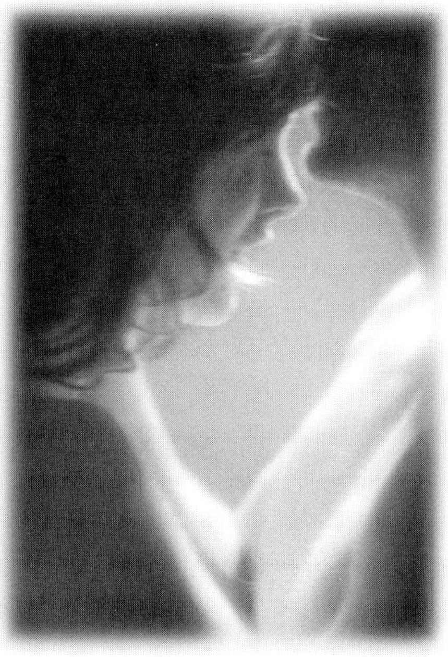

A Woman Like You

When you see me I'm in overalls
You're sitting at your desk, in a suit, taking calls
Who would imagine there could possibly be
Anything between
A woman like you and a man like me.

At first I was unaware you even saw me standing there
Emptying trash cans, taking care
Not to make too much noise because
Your work takes concentration.

Now I laugh when we love and you tell me to keep it down
In the office, you're used to doing things quietly
But me, I'm about to shout
Because I can't figure out why a woman like you
Shares her treasures with a man like me.

Darling, you say all good men are married
And I hope you'll understand my limitations
'Cause I haven't got a clue
How a married guy like me
Got so lucky with a single woman like you.

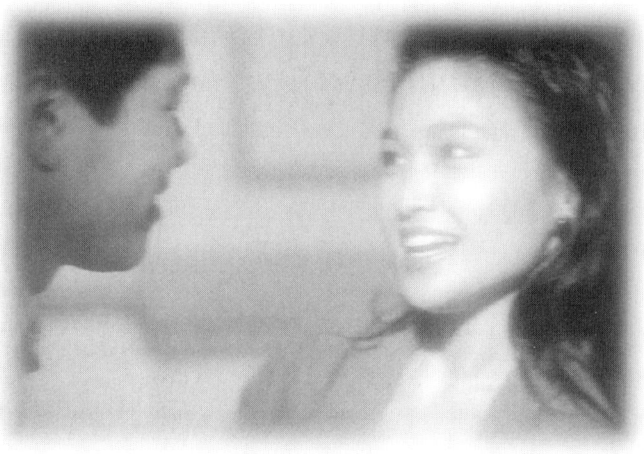

The Difference

'Why you?' she'd often say
As if the thought couldn't quite be put away
About why she cared as much as she did
And how she'd never rid herself of the one who made
The difference.

'Why you?' he'd say to himself
Smiling and looking into her exotic face
Some things cannot be explained, they are meant to remain
Mysteries
Out of which we learn to accept
The difference.

'Why you?' she'd ask
Expecting an answer she could understand
Concerning this change in the way she gave and expressed love
Above all they might suggest
The only one she would digest had to savor
The difference.

'Why you?' he dared not reason why
At his age he was given a chance to try
A love that came as a gift
Lifting him up and out of the rut he was in
Putting excitement in his life again
Everyone noticed
The difference.

The answer is, "Why not you?!"
For all the people and things too numerous to name
That are not the same
Vive la difference!

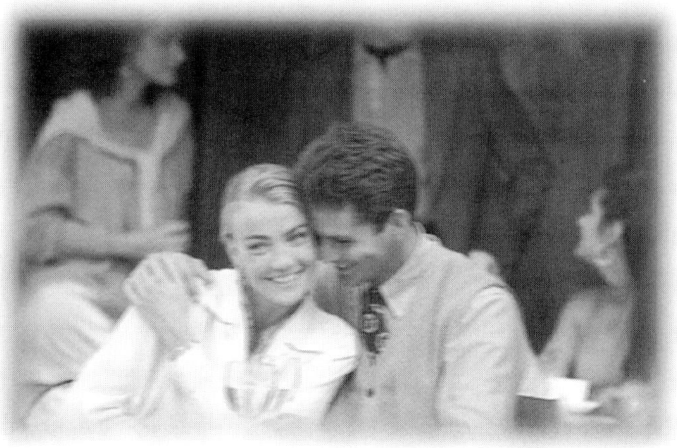

Does he notice....?

Does he notice the blush in your cheeks?
Does he notice how you've exercised for weeks
To get to the shape you're in?
Does he notice that you take more time for beauty's sake?
Does he notice your perfume when you enter the room?
Is he awake?
Does he notice how you fill every inch of your favorite blue dress?
Does he notice how well you handle success?

I do.

If ever you should tire of his absent-minded kisses,
Tire of all the time he must give to the missus
Tire of all the nights you spend alone, by the phone
Just remember this
You'll have all my attention, forget the hit or miss
Because I make it my business to notice.

The holiest of all holidays are those
Kept by ourselves in silence and apart;
The secret anniversaries of the heart.

— Henry Wadsworth Longfellow

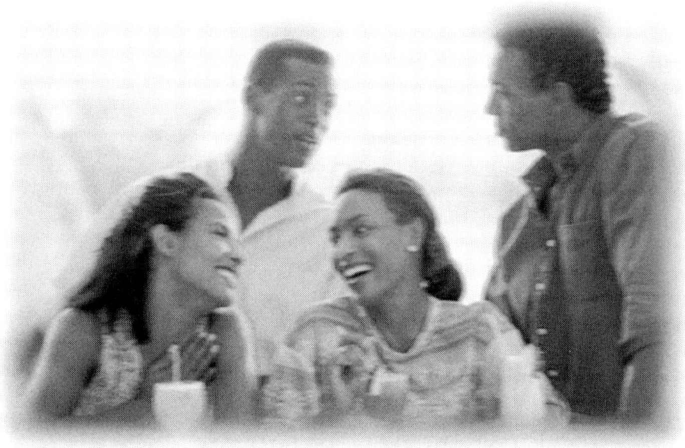

Holidays and Weekends

Used to love holidays and weekends
Times to relax and let down, spent with friends
But now all they are is a countdown until time away from you ends.

My closest friend, Alan, is the only one who knows
When I appear preoccupied where my thoughts go;
In my mind we can be together
Whenever and wherever I choose
Doesn't equal the real thing but it gets me through
The weekend, that seems to come around so fast,
If only our time together could seem as long to last.

It's a comfort to know you're also sad, thinking as I do
Misery like this needs company
What better partner in crime than you.
Thanksgiving and Christmas
Remind me, how thankful I am for the gift
Of a wonderful, special someone anxiously
Waiting, to share lusty love and secret sex.

Let's see, there are 104 Saturdays and Sundays
And eleven holidays to make us melancholy, too
Living two lives the way we do
Weekends and holidays, I spend time missing you.

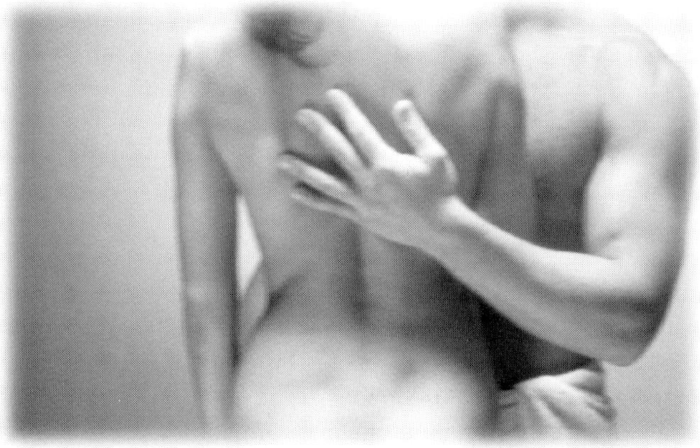

20 *lbs.*

I forgot to care about
Having grown so round
Nobody was asking for
My hand in marriage or
My body in bed
So why diet down 20 lbs?

Then, the right place
At the right time
A chance encounter
Made me remember
What's been forgot.
Agreed to, and see you
Over and over again.
With undivided attention
You have yet to mention
That I should diet down 20 lbs.

I know you're not staying
Not paying bills, raising my kids
Or giving me your name;
But there is something of value
I can happily claim:
Your caring way with me
More meaningful than it sounds
Was just the motivation I needed
To diet down 20 lbs.

There is nothing better for the spirit or the body than a love affair. It elevates the thoughts and flattens the stomachs.

— Barbara Howar

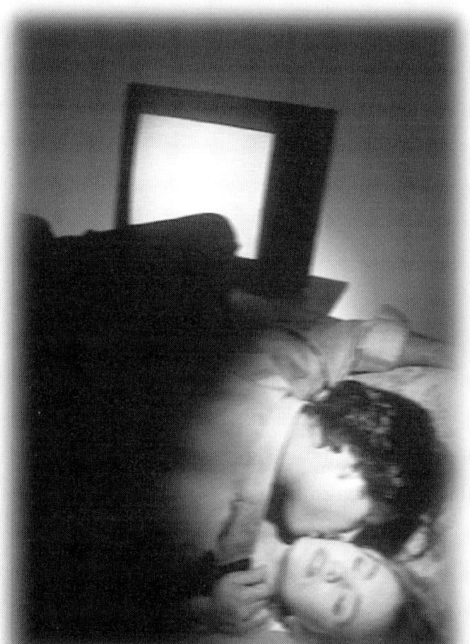

Younger Woman/Younger Man

Say what you will
Still want them young and
Firm of flesh
Conversation doesn't amount to much
Yet, we gush over the flower in bloom,
Bride and groom, forever young atop
The wedding cake.

And for the sake of ego she's out there looking
For a boy barely legal age
Thinking he can fix all that's wrong –
Can gauge the depth of her desire.
Surely the flames will glow brighter,
The fire burn hotter
When stoked by youthful hands.

Under the covers he discovers
Experience counts for much,
Makes up for a less than perfect body
Gently ravaged by time
In his prime, he learns and enjoys all he can
As a real woman makes a boy a man.

His hair has thinned, his girth turned thick
His is the voice of reason;
Wisdom's pearls fall with ease
And, "Any amount you need, I'm here to please,"
From the lips of the man she's teasing.

He knows all the right places to dine
Often falls asleep in his chair before nine
But she's patient with her father figure and terribly kind
To the older man who's teaching her to leave immaturity behind.

The rewards are many, why else would they be bothered?
Mothered or fathered
Toy boy or sweet thing
Is it win-win situations that such liaisons bring?

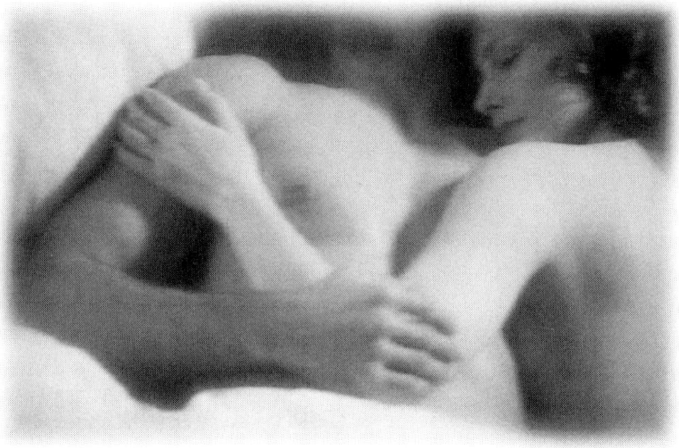

Not Guilty Enough

You seem to disapprove when I tell you truthfully
That I don't let a guilty conscience bother me.
I'm no hypocrite
I know what I'm out here to do, with you
So I won't say I feel bad
Just sad, watching you suffer
So here's the question I offer:
What good is guilt if it doesn't keep you at home?

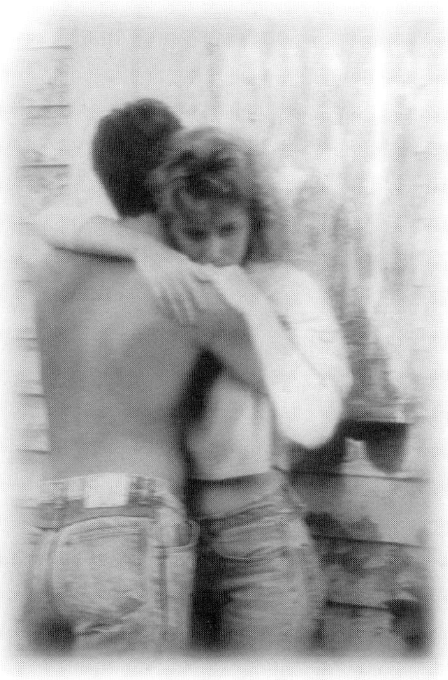

It's

(for Rose)

It's the way his hands rest on the wheel
When we're driving to our getaway
It's his strong arms around me
I remember the next day.

It's the whites of his eyes that make his tanned skin so pleasing
(Funny the things you notice for no apparent reason!)
It's the hair on his chest teasing out from his shirt
That makes me risk hurt
If we're ever found out.

It's the welcome in his smile when I enter the room
It's his laugh that makes me laugh and makes others
Assume he's all mine.
How could they know
That I will
Go home to someone else.

It's the presence of a man who knows his worth
It's new stories to remember about an angel here on earth
It's the tender squeeze of his hand
That signals what I understand
To mean I'm here, you can depend on to me.

It's the complete and utter surrender I allow
Myself in the protected embrace of the kind of man
I stopped believing was out there
After a lifetime with someone I now know never cared.

It's a heart that's willing to take me, problems and all
Away from this emptiness and pain
A parachute in a rescue mission that has helped me love again.

When a man steals your wife, there is no better revenge than to let him keep her.

— Sacha Guitry

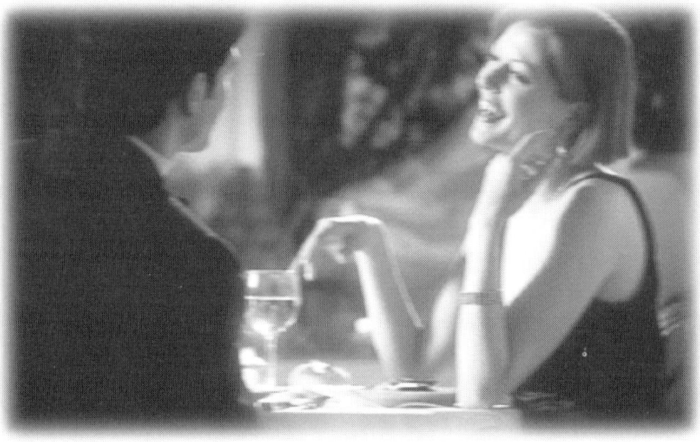

A Year From Now

"May I ask you a question?" she said.
(He wished she'd just go ahead and ask without permission)
But his response was, "By all means, start your inquisition."

"Well, do you think we'll be together
a year from now?"
(He wanted to say, "How would I know?"
But a patient man understands apprehension), so he replied,
"That's entirely up to you."

Then silence fell, and all seemed well until he spoke of travel.
"Tahiti is a mystery I really want to unravel," he was saying
"Take me with you," she exclaimed,
"How long will we be staying?"
(And just how would I do that? he thought
With wife and child to mollify)
So he just up and said, "Someday, maybe we'll try."

And for a while she simply smiled and said the sweetest things
Leaving alone that whiny tone that more queries would likely bring.
Inevitably, questions were the key to what she wanted most
So she started in all over again:
"May I ask you another question?"
(By now he was desperate, his mind shouting "No!" but avoiding hurt feelings),
He said instead
"Of course, go right ahead."

"Will your promise be to see only me, with no competition?"
(Does she really think I need any further aggravation? This question thing
Must depend on women's intuition
Otherwise, how can it be I'm so often in this position?
Between this one and my wife
I could spend my life
Answering silly questions!)

And so finally he said, "Listen, Honey, I've been thinking.
Perhaps the best thing to do
Is for me and you
To bring this conversation to a halt
Let's wait a year to continue this affair
By then maybe you'll have no more questions!"

When the glowing of passion's over,
and pinching winter comes,
will amorous sighs supply the
want of fire, or kind looks and kisses
keep off hunger?

— Susannah Centlivre
The Artiface Act V

I will not be cheated — nor will I employ long
years of repentance for moments of joy.

— Mary Wortley Montagu
*Comment to [Alexander] Pope,
Quoted in History of English Literature
by Jeremy Collier*

He was my North, my South, my East and West,
My working week and Sunday rest,
My noon, my midnight, my talk, my song;
I thought that love would last forever: I was wrong.

— W. H. Auden

Drink, and dance and laugh and lie,
Love the reeling midnight through,
For tomorrow we shall die!
(But, alas, we never do.)

— Dorothy Parker,
'The Flaw in Paganism'

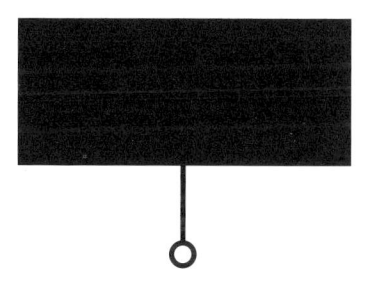

In the end...

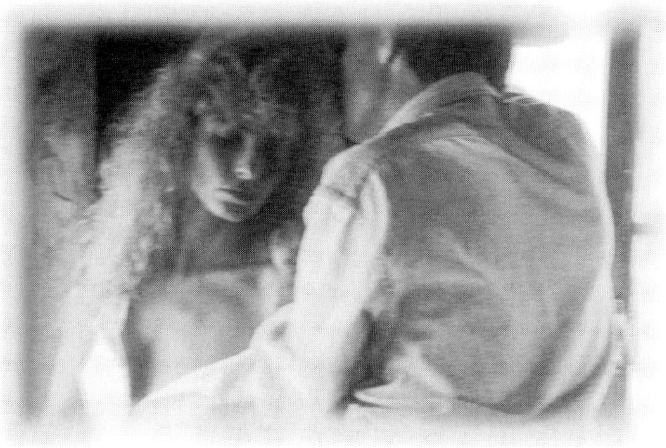

With You In The Room It's Even More Empty

I've faced the fact you'll never love me like I want you to
You mouth the words but saying them doesn't make it so
Your intention isn't committing to any real feeling
Secret sex on the side is all that's appealing.

I'll get over losing you
It's clear you don't intend to stay
I see you and then I don't
You'll call and then you won't
No doubt it's just a matter of time.

Lately you're distracted, hardly able to discuss
Ideas, events, situations that were once important to us
It's as if we no longer have anything in common
Except that we're involved in
An unhappy affair.

With you in the room it's even more empty
Moody silences, unloving words
Create distance between us
Do you intend to force my hand, make me ask you for my key?
Sorry, I won't make it easy for you to walk away from me.

You're going to have to say those dreaded words
And go back to the life of phony respectability you've led
With a partner who hasn't a clue that the real you
Is a cheat – just like me.

Nought but vast sorrow was there —
The sweet cheat gone.

— Walter de la Mare
The Ghost

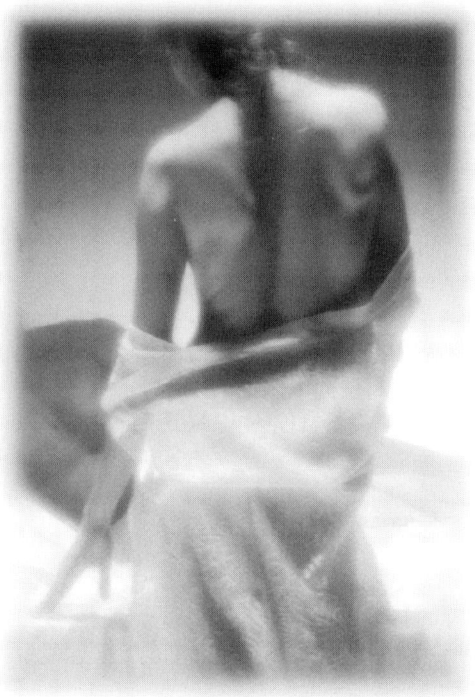

Can't Cheat A Cheater

It's taken time to dry my tears
This affair's gone on for several years
Your word, my word, all a matter of trust,
Through all the hiding, sneaking and danger
It was you and me alone, just us.

Now that's no longer so
And I'm angry, I want revenge
I could call your wife and tell her
What a two-timing cheat you've been,
But, I won't hurt that woman again.

I've got to find a way to bring you to your knees
When I'm done I intend to be the one who's totally pleased.

Your adversary let me know on more than one occasion
A look, a touch, never said too much, but made it clear
He'd be a better diversion.
That's it!
I'll tell him all the secrets you've been hiding
Tell him he's the better man,
Rather be the object of his affection.

His sense of competition made it easy to execute my plan
What he didn't know was that I'd designed a surprise for you, Mr. Man!
Took him to our place, the one we shared, far away from home
Toward the end of our stay, your key turned in the lock at the door
As it opened, your enemy you saw first
Seeing me standing behind him made matters worse.
I'll always remember the look on your face
As you stood on the threshold of our little love nest
Your huge ego deflated, you'd been replaced.

I've never seen either of you again and I don't regret the fact
That revenge was all mine in one cunningly duplicitous act!

...spite will make a woman do more than love...

> — Margaret of Navarre
> *Novel II, the first day,*
> *The Heptameron, or Novels of the*
> *Queen of Navarre 1558*

You can't buy love, but you can pay heavily for it.

> — Henny Youngman

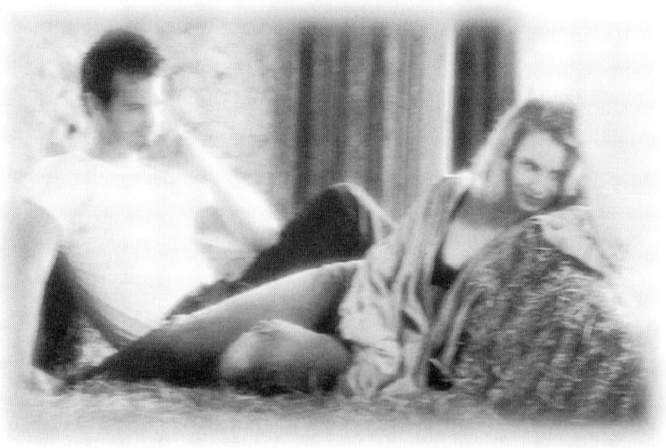

Heartburn

He loved her
But wouldn't tell her so
She loved him
But thought about letting go.
Putting little trust in an unseen future
They ventured no further
Down mystery's road.
Married, he believed he knew
What was for the best
Divorced, she hadn't had the answers
Failed the test.
Two sad people
Never discerning whether
They could have known love
Together.

Ships that pass in the night, and speak each other in passing,
  Only a signal shown, and a distant voice in the darkness.
  So on the ocean of life we pass and speak one another.
  Only a look and a voice; then darkness again and a silence.

— Henry Wadsworth Longfellow
Tales of a Wayside Inn

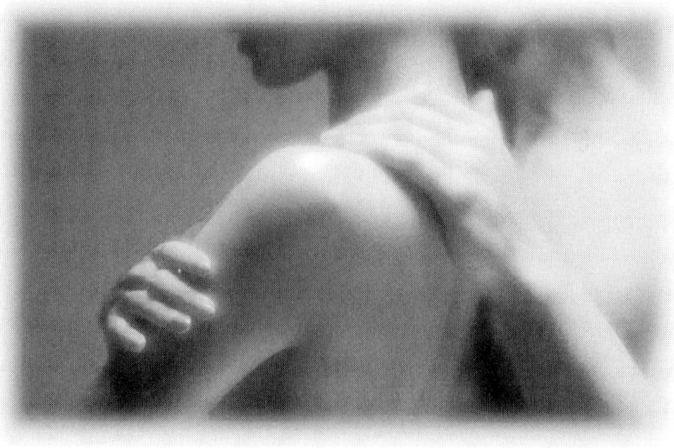

Next Lifetime

Sorry that I can't stay
I have to go back home
My family needs me
Can't walk away
From responsibility to the man
Who loves me so and doesn't know...
Listen, I've really got to go
In my dreams you'll always be part
Of the most precious things in my heart
Happy to have been in love with you
Glad to know what's in store
I fully intend to be with you again
When we'll both be free
Please arrange it for me in
Our next lifetime

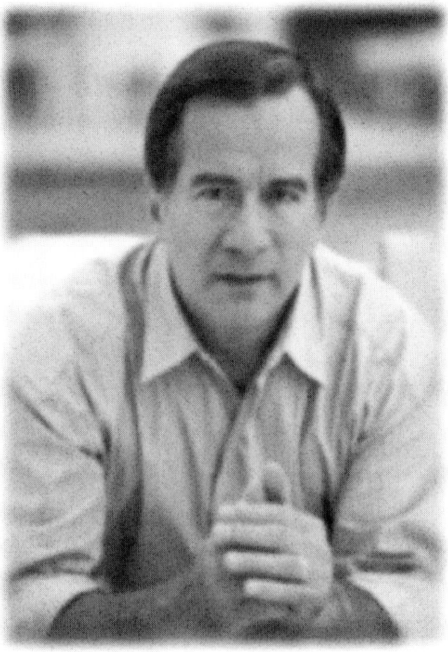

Disconnected

Since Wednesday
She stopped telephoning
Hasn't returned any of my calls
No, we didn't have a fight
Could be somebody found out
About our little fling

Think I better get on home
Sure hope my wife hasn't heard anything!

Matrimony! ha, ha, ha! what
Crimes have you committed against the
God of Love that he should revenge 'em so
severely to stamp Husband upon your
Forehead?

— Susannah Centlivre
The Busy Body

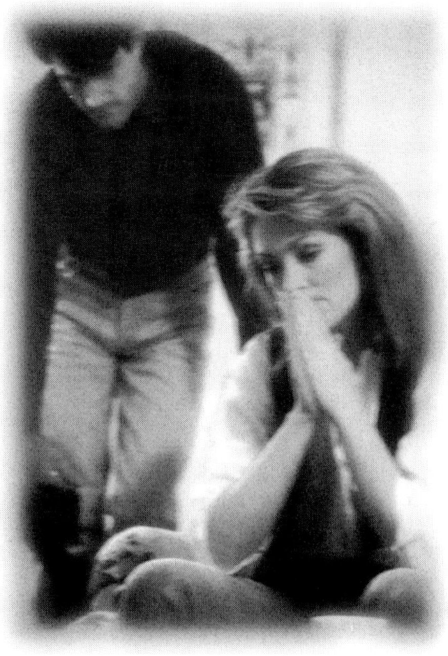

"...but you're my best friend!"

It's not like I don't know how this happened
I knew what I was doing,
I wanted some stolen, sweet, secret wooing
From a man I knew would be just right.
Wanted no more impressing
Men I didn't know, tired of the flow of traffic through my house,
Looking for a spouse but only finding fault;
Needed to put a halt to all that hullabaloo.
Confronted with all this, she'll likely insist
"...but you're my best friend!"

Since we were kids our choices were the same:
"Give me vanilla, too...
I wanna be in the game with you."
Her favorite color, lavender, decorated my bedroom walls
Long, late night phone calls
Were always full of common purpose.
That's why she'd understand why I would want the man she chose.
How could she suppose it would be any other way?
Even so I know she'd say "...but you're my best friend!"

As much as I want you, I've got to do what's right,
End this deception tonight
For the sake of the friend who thinks so much of me,
And for whom I need to be
A best friend.

Can't continue to be part of a "we" that would break her heart.

Last Best Day

Everything was perfect, couldn't have been better
That's why I cried so when I got his letter
'It was the best it's ever been. Let's end it on that note,
So we can remember the loving, wonderful way
We spent our time together,'
Was his suggestion.

I couldn't see it that way at first, but perhaps in time
I'll see the good in his approach
But it doesn't take the pain away
Or mend a heart that's breaking
It was a clean break the decent man I loved was making.

For this is Wisdom; to love, to live
To take what fate, or the Gods may give.
To ask no question, to make no prayer,
To kiss the lips and caress the hair,
Speed passion's ebb as you greet its flow
To have, – to hold – and – in time, – let go!

— Laurence Hope

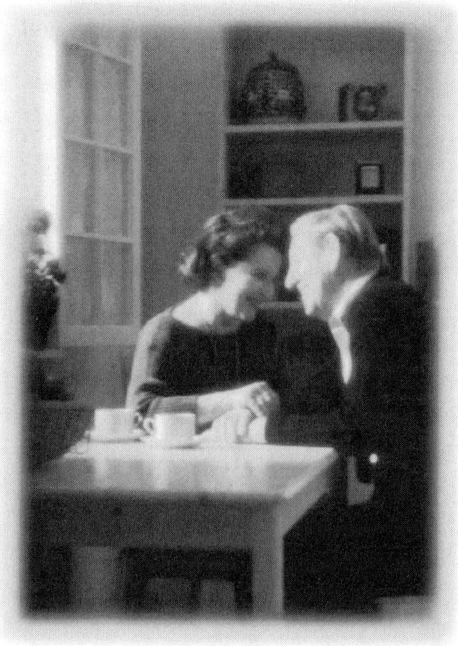

Promised Land

From the beginning
It was useless to try to convince her
Otherwise
She loved him, believed in him, no one else would ever do
No compromise was possible, to him she remained true.

The first year was pure magic, the second fantasy
The third a dream come true
He gave his commitment to leave home, wife and kids, too.

Never having married, she had no idea of happily ever after
No disappoints, no loss, no unresolved anger
She couldn't know what it meant to break a bond so strong
How delicate the situation when breaking hearts
The false starts the guilty make
And all else at stake
In an effort to make a promise real.

But she was a kind woman, not one to take offense
Just couldn't make sense of his continued reluctance
Kept it to herself, put her future on the shelf
Made every moment pleasure when they were together.

For nineteen years she kept herself desirable, always well groomed
A demure demeanor
Fresh flowers in each room
No kids around to disturb champagne in a candlelit tub
Waterlogged love, a soothing back rub
No part left out
Sheer will kept her going when his promises stopped
You can only suppose her a fool or that she knew something we did not.

He helped her pick out furnishings, shopped for groceries and such
He guided her career taking little, giving much
While she kept love alive when it might have died
Had she made the smarter move.

The day she died, he wept aloud, tears staining her hand
Declaring through love and life with her he'd reached the 'promised land'.

I believe that if I should die,
and you were to walk near my grave,
from the very depths of the earth
I would hear your footsteps.

—Benito Perez Galdos

When I am dead, my dearest,
Sing no sad songs for me:
Plant thou no roses at my head,
Nor shady cypress tree.
Be the green grass above me
With showers and dewdrops wet:
And if thou wilt, remember
And if thou wilt, forget.

— Christina Rossetti
Song